Serving Others:
A Short Read to
Transform Your Heart

YOU'RE IMPORTANT, SO SERVE

HERMAN BAXTER JR.

Published by Royalty Lane Publishing

You're Important, So Serve
By Herman Baxter Jr.

Copyright © 2024 Herman Baxter Jr.

All rights reserved. No part of this publication may be reproduced, distributed, or transmitted in any form or by any means, including photocopying, recording, or other electronic or mechanical methods, without the prior written permission of the publisher, except in the case of brief quotations embodied in critical reviews and certain other noncommercial uses permitted by copyright law.

Scripture quotations have been taken from the Christian Standard Bible®, copyright © 2017 by Holman Bible Publishers. Used by permission. Christian Standard Bible® and CSB® are federally registered trademarks of Holman Bible Publishers.

Jacket Design: Humble Books
Book Design: Humble Books

ISBN 13 TP: 979-8-218-60701-2

Contents

Introduction 7

You're Important, But It's About Christ 13

You're Important, So Lovingly Serve with Family 27

You're Important, So Add Value 37

You're Important, So Be Healthy 53

Introduction

MY FATHER SERVED in the United States Air Force for over twenty-five years, and I grew up on Air Force bases for the first decade of my life. I remember the sounds of jets slicing through the air and seeing men and women in blue or green uniforms walking with purpose. I even had the privilege of going to work with my dad a few times while he examined various weaponry and aircraft.

Although I have amazing memories of life on different Air Force bases, what I remember most are the Air Force core values my father and Air Force ROTC taught me: integrity first, service before self, and excellence in all we do. I admit, I would impress many employers by quoting the core values when I was trying to get jobs in my teenage years, even though my work habits rarely reflected the values. However, as I matured by gaining life experience and work experience, watching the lives of mentors, and more importantly, giving my life to Christ, my decisions and actions showed the values far better than me just reciting them. Although I am not perfect, I was the one willing to take the initiative, help others, and admit to making mistakes without passing blame at work or where I served. Why did my work and service now support the values I would quote? Because of a heart and head change.

As Christians, it is common to develop what I call "Rote Christianity" when it comes to serving. "Rote Christianity" is when followers of Christ live what they know from Scripture out of pure habit, training, or memory but not necessarily with understanding and sincerity. I am not saying developing habits, doing what was taught, or memorizing is wrong. What I am saying is that through the ebbs and flows of the Christian life, there should be consistent growth for loving people and loving Christ that makes the aspects of our Christian walk more than just boxes to check off. This book addresses the aspect of serving and will help bring understanding of why and how we should serve as followers of Christ. And, prayerfully, from this understanding we begin or continue to serve with sincerity. My hope is that the Lord will accomplish a heart and head change in you, the reader.

Jesus says, "The harvest is abundant, but the workers are few" (Matthew 9:37), and many local churches can attest to this. The congregation steadily grows, but the number of volunteers remains the same or dwindles. Those who are serving begin to feel overwhelmed and possibly begin to burn out. Leaders become burdened because they constantly need to recruit new volunteers on top of executing their duties and leading their teams. The list goes on. So what should we do since workers are few? Jesus says, "Pray to the Lord of the harvest to send out workers into His harvest" (Matthew 9:38). Now, what do you do when our Lord answers the prayer? This book serves the purpose of being a resource once the Lord sends the workers.

In America, we live in a culture where the individual is seen as important and community is secondary (*community* meaning the local community or society in general). People's mindset leans toward what the community can do for me, rather than what I can do for my community. I agree that everyone has a level of importance. We are all made in the image of God and have value. However, our individual importance should not be to the detriment of the community. Scripture says in Philippians 2:3, "Consider others more important than yourselves." And Romans 12:10 says to "lead in honoring one another." These verses communicate that we should see the importance of others as much or more than our own importance. Likewise, other people should see your importance too. But because we are important, our community needs us to serve in love with humility and joy. Let's explore how this book will help.

In the first chapter, we'll see that even though we are important, serving is about Christ. Our work has historical and eternal significance. We have the opportunity to change lives here on earth and reap eternal rewards in heaven. Nevertheless, Jesus is still the *why* behind our efforts. His glory and His Kingdom are of the utmost importance and focus. In chapter 2, we look at how we are important, so we should lovingly serve with family. Christians have been adopted into the family of God. We are brothers and sisters in Christ. Therefore, we should be ecstatic to serve and spend time with one another. Sadly, many church members experience hurt while serving others or burnout because no one seems to want to help. A loving family goes all out to help one another. A loving family fights for relationships. A loving family shows humility.

Chapter 3 explores how we're important and that God gives us different gifts and abilities, so we should add value to where we serve. We should look for needs to help in and out of the four walls of the church, actively pursue opportunities to grow in our gifts, and display leadership qualities even without an official title. The final chapter talks about recognizing that we're important, so we need to be healthy Christians. We explore what it means to be healthy and what actions to take so that we serve in a healthy way and help develop a healthy serving culture.

INTRODUCTION

My hope and prayer is that you find joy in serving and that your local church begins to see more people develop the heart to serve. We have the unique privilege of being ambassadors of Christ. We get to represent Him where we live, work, play, and serve. We get to have a small part in the trajectory of people's lives. The way we serve is instrumental because God can use our service to transform our communities and our world. Are you ready? Let's go.

CHAPTER 1

You're Important, But It's About Christ

BASKETBALL IS MY FAVORITE SPORT. Growing up, I would play all the time. I remember grabbing a rebound and hitting the winning shot when I was seven. I also started collecting hundreds of NBA basketball cards around that same time. When I lived on an Air Force base with my dad, some of my best moments were at the recreational center playing basketball. My love of basketball remains to this day. And boldly, in the ever-ongoing debate, I stand by my thoughts since 1995: Michael Jordan is the greatest basketball player of all time.

I grew up a Chicago Bulls fan, so of course, MJ

would be my favorite player. So whom would I try to imitate whenever I played basketball? Even without physically seeing me, you can imagine a young kid shooting fadeaway shots and going for layups with my tongue out. I took the Gatorade commercial to heart; I wanted to be like Mike. As I matured as a basketball player, I had to develop a unique playing style (I'm nowhere near 6-foot-6, and I'm less athletic). Still, Michael Jordan's style and mindset molded the way I played basketball.

Think about your interests. Are there great people you try to imitate? For baseball, it could be Derek Jeter or Clayton Kershaw. You may enjoy cooking, so you look to Rachael Ray or Gordon Ramsay. There may be people unknown to the masses whom you look up to. In any case, greatness is attractive and successful, so we naturally want to mimic the greatness we see. If you could master that one shot, painting style, or way of speaking, you could have the same impact as the one you want to imitate.

Whether you know it or not, if you serve or you are thinking about serving in the local church, you have greatness to imitate. You have the most significant person to imitate that has ever walked this planet. That person is none other than Jesus Christ Himself. Now, you may be wondering what Jesus has to do with serving in your local church. If you are a believer, I'm sure you've heard that you are to be Christlike. We should love as He loved, tell people about Him, and share the Gospel as He did. But what if you only help clean the church and set up furniture? Or you only greet once a month? Or you only pass out snacks in the children's ministry? What does being great and being like Jesus have to do with those things? I'm glad you asked.

You're Important . . .

First, let's remove the word *only* from your mind. If you think and verbalize that you *only* serve in areas that seem less glamorous than singing or preaching, you are lowering your value and the value of that ministry. As a person, you have value because you are created in the image of God, or the *imago dei* (Genesis 1:26). As a believer in Christ, you have value because He has given you new life and a new identity (2 Corinthians 5:17). As someone who is serving, you have value because God has given you gifts that are needed (1 Peter 4:10). Do not demean yourself, your contributions, and the ministry you serve in.

. . . But It's about Christ

We began this chapter by talking about imitating greatness and saying that Jesus is the person we should imitate. It helps to know a little about the person we're trying to emulate. I never want to assume that just because you serve in the church or you're thinking about serving, you know who Jesus is. Moreover, we shouldn't just know who He is; we must also understand why serving is ultimately about Christ. Let's dive in!

Jesus Who?

Jesus is God, the second person of the Trinity, which includes the Father and Holy Spirit. Jesus is eternal, meaning He was not created; He has always been, and He was active in creation (John 8:56–58; Colossians 1:15–18). Jesus wrapped Himself in human flesh and was born a child (Genesis 3:15; Isaiah 7:14; Matthew 1:22–25). Jesus, the Messiah or Chosen One, grew up with the Father's grace on Him and in wisdom, stature, and favor with the Father and people (Luke 2:40, 52). At the appointed time, Jesus was baptized by John the Baptist, was led by the Holy Spirit to be tempted, and began His public ministry (Mark 1:9–15).

The account of Jesus found in the Gospels, Mark, Matthew, Luke, and John, provides four portraits of Jesus. One story told from four different perspectives. Mark describes Jesus as the Suffering Servant or Suffering Son of God. In Matthew, we see Jesus as the Messiah and King. Luke tells the story of Jesus as the Son of Man or Savior of all people. And John depicts Jesus as the Son of God or the Son who reveals the Father.[1] For this chapter, we'll look at Christ through the lens of Mark to see the greatness of His servitude and why we should imitate Him no matter where we serve.

---

1 A great resource about Jesus and the Gospels is *Four Portraits, One Jesus* by Mark L. Strauss (Grand Rapids, MI: Zondervan, 2007).

How Did Jesus Serve on Earth?

Jesus is known by many, both Christians and non-believers, for His good works on earth. The general consensus, for those who believe Jesus is a historical figure, is that He was a great teacher who loved everyone He came in contact with. While this is true, this description falls short of the entire truth. The fact is that Jesus is more than a great teacher. He is God, who came to earth on a mission to restore the relationship between His creation and Himself. The Gospel of Mark tells His story in two main parts: the first is about Jesus showing His authority, and the second focuses on Jesus being the Suffering Servant. In the first part, we see Jesus serve by performing many miracles, like healing the sick, exorcising demons, and raising the dead. These actions are dual-purposeful. They reveal His authority as the Messiah, and through them He is serving His people. In the second half of Mark, we see Jesus teach more about His impending suffering and why He came to earth. We follow Him on the way to Jerusalem, where He will demonstrate the ultimate act of service—giving His life on the cross.

So how did He serve on earth? First, He met the needs He encountered. In the first chapter of Mark, Jesus encounters someone with an unclean spirit, Simon's ill mother-in-law, and a man with leprosy. Jesus did not tell them He needed time to pray about helping them. He did not ponder if it was His calling to help these people. Jesus encountered a need and served the people to help with that need. We often overcomplicate serving in the local church; more often than not, we simply need to meet a need. We should simply do what is right and good. So, seeing the needs of these people, Jesus did what was right and met the needs of each one. He exorcised the unclean spirit, healed Simon's mother-in-law of her fever, and cleansed the man of his leprosy. All in the first chapter! These actions continue throughout the Gospel as Jesus shows us that if we can meet a need, then we should meet that need.

Jesus also served by sacrificing. Mark 1:35–38 constantly challenges me. The Scripture passage says, "Very early in the morning, while it was still dark, he got up, went out, and made his way to a deserted place; and there he was praying. Simon and his companions searched for him, and when they found him they said, 'Everyone is looking for you.' And he said to them, 'Let's go on to the neighboring villages so that I may preach there too. This is why I have come.' "

Do you understand the sacrifice He made? You might have missed it because we did not examine the verses before verse 35. After Jesus healed Simon's mother-in-law, verses 32–34 reveal that when it was evening people brought "all those who were sick and demon-possessed" and that "the whole town was assembled at the door." And you know what Jesus did? Scripture says, "He healed many who were sick . . . and drove out many demons." Do you see it? Jesus was up through the evening serving people, He woke up early in the morning to spend time in prayer, and then He went to serve people again through preaching. Not only that, but if you read on, He also continues to serve by healing more people!

Notice that He did not choose to sleep in, although He served late. Notice He did not skip out on prayer. Notice He did not tell the disciples He's relaxing because He served all day yesterday. Jesus sacrificed His time to serve. Now, I know what you may be thinking. Jesus is God; He has supernatural energy. Jesus didn't have a full-time job. Jesus did not have kids to raise. I understand. I'm not saying burn yourself out (more on that later in this book). I'm not saying not to consider your job when serving. I'm not saying neglect family to serve in the local church. But my question to you is this: What are you willing to sacrifice to serve? I once heard that following Christ is not complicated; it's costly. Did you count the cost of following Christ? How are you choosing to be more selfless and less selfish with your time, talent, and treasure? Does sacrifice and giving things up even come to your mind when thinking about serving and being like Christ? Let's skip ahead in the Gospel of Mark and see where we stand.

> What are you willing to sacrifice to serve?

Sacrifice, Serving, Greatness

As a basketball fan, I needed to own a copy of *The Mamba Mentality* by Kobe Bryant. Kobe is my second-favorite basketball player, and I tried to mimic some elements of his game too (he was very similar to MJ, so there was not much change). I remember that one day I was watching TV when a Sprite commercial came on. Kobe was lifting weights, running, and practicing basketball, all while drinking Sprite. So, being an impressionable middle school kid, I was trying to imitate greatness, and I had the grand idea to drink Sprite while I played basketball. If Kobe does it and plays at that level, I should do it too. The next time I went to the recreational center after school, I made sure I had a ball and Sprite in my hand. After shooting around for a while and playing a couple of games, Charley struck me. No, Charley was not another basketball player. It was a charley horse cramp in my calf caused by dehydration. Thanks, Sprite, and thanks, Kobe.

In all seriousness, Kobe's book *The Mamba Mentality* provides excellent insight into his work ethic, mentality, and sacrifices to reach greatness. For example, Kobe writes that if he began workouts at 5 a.m., he could train and have extra workouts in a day and still have time for family. He states, "I wasn't willing to sacrifice my game, but I also wasn't willing to sacrifice my family time. So I decided to sacrifice sleep, and that was that."[2] Well, his sacrifice speaks for itself: five-time champion, eighteen-time all-star, MVP, two-time Finals MVP, and two retired jerseys are just a few of his accolades. What did it take to achieve such greatness? He had to make sacrifices. He chose to let go of some things to attain something greater.

A well-known passage of Scripture regarding sacrifice, service, and greatness is in Mark 10. We find Jesus speaking to His disciples in verse 35, after two of them, James and John, have made a bold request. They ask Jesus if they may sit at His right and left hand in glory, a sign of greatness. Jesus doesn't condemn their desire to be great, but He challenges their perspective on how to reach greatness. Jesus first contrasts earthly greatness and Kingdom greatness by stating that "Gentiles lord it over [others], and those in high positions act as tyrants" (verse 42). In contrast to earthly greatness, Jesus proclaims that "whoever wants to become great among you will be your servant.... For even the Son of Man did not come to be served, but to serve, and to give his life as a ransom for many" (verses 43, 45). Jesus is saying that if you want to be great, you will serve others. Also, we are to look to Him as the example, because He has come to serve us in the ultimate way: taking our place on the cross and dying for the sins of humanity.

---

[2] Kobe Bryant, *The Mamba Mentality: How I Play* (New York: Farrar, Straus and Giroux, 2018), 26.

YOU'RE IMPORTANT, BUT IT'S ABOUT CHRIST

However, to fully capture the idea of sacrifice, let's go back to the beginning of Mark's chapter to an encounter with a rich young ruler. In verse 17, this young ruler confidently but curiously approached Jesus and asked how he could inherit eternal life. I say confidently because Jesus asked him if he had kept the commandments of the law, and the young ruler proclaimed, "Teacher, I have kept all these from my youth" (verse 20). Interestingly, Jesus had listed the commandments that deal with horizontal relationships or loving your neighbor. Desiring to reveal the young man's heart, Jesus responded to the question with practical steps. Verse 21 tells us that Jesus told him to sell everything he had to the poor and that he'd have treasure in heaven, and then to follow Jesus. E-ve-ry-thing? E-ve-ry-thing.

This rich young ruler walked away dismayed and grieving because that's a hard demand. That is a huge sacrifice! Admittedly, this could be a challenging passage to connect with. We have more than most people globally in America, but most Americans certainly would not consider themselves rich or rulers. But we still know that giving up what money we do have would be tough. Shifting our thoughts beyond money, what else are we unwilling to sacrifice to follow and be like Christ? For this young ruler, he was unwilling to sacrifice possessions to become like Jesus. Think about church service and the sacrifice it takes to serve.

Maybe you love comfort too much. Your time may be sacred. Being in church often means missing some NFL games or other shows. But Jesus shows us that following Him, being like Him, and ultimately living where He lives forever requires sacrifice. Remember that in Mark 10:45, Jesus stated that He came to serve. If we're Christlike, we will aim to do what He did. Sacrifice, service, and greatness go hand in hand. Let's put this all together. Like the rich young ruler, we must sacrifice our time, talent, and treasure to follow and be like Jesus. Being like Jesus is to mimic greatness, because He is the greatest being ever. And to mimic greatness means being servants.

> If we're Christlike, we will aim to do what He did.

Serving Is about Christ

Although we serve others, we do it for the glory of our Lord and Savior, Jesus Christ. Jesus came to earth to serve, and He expects us to serve the people around us, but we are to serve so that eyes and hearts turn to the One who gave His all to save them. *Coram mundo* describes active righteousness toward other people (1 Peter 4:10; Matthew 25:31–40). It is defined by righteous deeds and service to humanity. It is a horizontal righteousness. Christian rapper Flame likes to say that our neighbor needs our good works, not God.

We should use our time, talents, and treasure for the benefit of others. But what gives good works eternal value is faith in Christ. For those who are serving, I hope you have declared Jesus as Lord and Savior because you have received righteousness from God, or *coram deo*. *Coram deo* is passive righteousness that we cannot earn by good works; it is given by God through faith in Christ (Romans 3:21–22). This is vertical righteousness. So, as you serve, you can have confidence that you are not attempting to earn right standing with God, but you serve for the betterment of your neighbor fulfilling the primary commands (Mark 12:29–31).

> *Coram mundo* is defined by righteous deeds & service to humanity.

When you serve others, you must remember you're doing it as stewards of your given abilities, through faith in Christ, for His glory, leading people to worship Him. As a greeter, you welcome congregants into church, believing they will encounter Christ that day. If you serve food, you joyously feed people, believing that their body and soul will be nourished by Christ. If you set up furniture, you believe people will gather and experience the incomparable presence of Christ and be transformed. Your belief is that the triune God is working in and through you to accomplish His desire that no one should perish (2 Peter

3:9) and that the people you serve see your good works and give glory to God (Matthew 5:16). I think the apostle Peter sums up this section better when he says, "Just as each one has received a gift, use it to serve others, as good stewards of the varied grace of God. If anyone speaks, let it be as one who speaks God's words; if anyone serves, let it be from the strength God provides, so that God may be glorified through Jesus Christ in everything. To him be the glory and the power forever and ever. Amen" (1 Peter 4:10–11).

> *Coram deo* is passive righteousness that we cannot earn by good works

CHAPTER 2

You're Important, So Lovingly Serve with Family

I WANT YOU TO IMAGINE something with me. Let's say you are married (for those who are, this exercise may be easier for you), and, as expected, you are extremely in love with your spouse. Head over heels, sprung, crazy in love. They're not perfect, of course, but they have your eyes and heart. Now, picture yourself having a wonderful time with your spouse at a gathering with friends, family, and other guests. You walk alone to a circle of friends and family and begin talking about life. The topic of marriage comes up, and

YOU'RE IMPORTANT, SO LOVINGLY SERVE WITH FAMILY

you mention your spouse. Then one of your family members says, "You know, I'm not really fond of your spouse. Honestly, they don't really look that great, and I feel like they're hypocritical at times." Feeling bold, one of your friends decides to speak up too. "I like you, and I'll hang with you any day, but your spouse, I don't know."

Pause here. What's going through your mind? How would you feel? How would you respond?

This kind of situation happens with the church all the time. The catholic church (not to be confused with the Roman Catholic church; *catholic* means universal) is described as the Bride of Christ (Revelation 19:7–9), and Christ loves His Bride. How much does He love the Bride? Ephesians 5:25 tells us that He "gave himself for her" by leaving paradise, living the perfect life, humbling Himself to mocking, beating, whipping, spitting, and death on a cross, and then ultimately rose again so He can "present the church to Himself in splendor, without spot or wrinkle or anything like that, but holy and blameless" (verse 27). So what about our example above; where do we see this situation play out? When people say things like "I love Jesus, but not the church," or "It's my personal relationship with Jesus; I don't need church." Sisters and brothers, this is not how it should be. If we genuinely have the same Spirit (Ephesians 4:4), we should love the church, faults and all.

YOU'RE IMPORTANT, SO LOVINGLY SERVE WITH FAMILY

Our perspective of the local church must change. I'm not ignorant of the fact that church hurt is real. Some churches have bad, deceitful, manipulative pastors and leaders. There are members of churches who are just as hypocritical, gossipy, messy, and rude as people who do not know Christ. I understand the hurt and pain you may have experienced. I pray for your healing and the rescue of individuals within those four walls. Nevertheless, we must all remember a few things to see the local church as Christ sees the church. First, this is why the Gospel is the most essential truth. Jesus died for their sins just as much as yours and mine. Just as we have received grace and forgiveness, so we must give the same. It may not happen immediately; healing can take time, and forgiving others is not always easy. But Christians forgive just as Christ forgives us.

Second, we are family. My kids are seven and nine as I write this book, and we love watching the Trolls movies. The Trolls series follows the life of singing trolls who go on adventures, and the songs are fantastic! The latest film focuses on one of the main characters, Branch, as he reunites with his long-lost brothers. They were a singing group that disbanded and did not speak to one another for many years. In an early scene, one of Branch's older brothers finds him and reveals he is, in fact, one of his brothers. Quickly, Branch proclaims that he is not his brother anymore and tells Poppy that he's his former brother. Poppy, another main character, emphatically rebuttals that DNA does not work that way. I share that scene because we as believers can act like other Christians are not our family because personalities clash or they've hurt us. Well, that's not how the blood of Christ works!

Scripture often tells us that the church is family (see Ephesians 1:5; Galatians 3:26). Just like with your biological family, you don't get to pick your spiritual family. The beautiful and broken church consists of personalities, struggles, and gifts. Nevertheless, we should serve and love one another. In John 13, Jesus is with the disciples and does something remarkable. Jesus, God in the flesh, washes their feet! That is one of the lowest things to do in that society, yet Jesus willingly does it. Moreover, He says, "So if I, your Lord and Teacher, have washed your feet, you also ought to wash one another's feet. For I have given you an example, that you also should do just as I have done for you" (verses 14–15). Furthermore, in the same scene toward the end of the chapter, Jesus commands, "Love one another. Just as I have loved you, you are also to love one another" (verse 34).

Sisters and brothers, we established that we are to imitate Christ and mimic His greatness by sacrificing and serving. We serve with love because Christ loves His Bride, the church. You are part of this universal church that He profoundly loves, so yes, He loves you too. Furthermore, He's looking to present the Bride spotless without wrinkles. We have a part to play in that, and serving with family is one way we do our part.

You're Important . . .

Another metaphor for the universal church is a body. For example, Paul refers to Christians as the Body of Christ in Romans 12:5 and 1 Corinthians 12:12–13. The church as a body is an amazing thought. Just like the physical body relies on many parts to function correctly, Christ's church is the same. No matter how hard I try, I cannot make my hands see anything; I must have my eyes. My feet can get me places, but I need my kidneys to filter blood, something my feet cannot do. Every part of my body works together so I can live and function.

Similarly, the universal and local church needs everyone to function according to Christ's instructions. We need one another. Your church needs you. You may have a special gift to organize, clean, make people feel welcome, discern problems, or fix anything broken. Use them for the church! In 1 Corinthians 12:21–24, Paul states, "The eye cannot say to the hand, 'I don't need you!' Or again, the head can't say to the feet, 'I don't need you!' On the contrary, those parts of the body that are weaker are indispensable. And those parts of the body that we consider less honorable, we clothe these with greater honor, and our unrespectable parts are treated with greater respect, which our respectable parts do not need." No matter how small or unimportant you think the role or skill is, I encourage you to press past those thoughts and serve. The church needs what God has given you.

. . . So Lovingly Serve with Family

The Book of Acts is a narrative by Luke describing the early church. Conversions, miracles, teachings, persecution, and missionary journeys are found in its pages. In Acts 2, Scripture reveals that the early church grew in number and was filled with generosity, love, and community. They had all things in common, sold possessions and distributed them amongst themselves, met together every day in the temple, and hung out afterward in different homes (verses 44–47). However, these loving, truthful acts are not isolated to the Bible. The Bible speaks of history, and history tells the same story. In the third century, Tertullian, a theologian known as the father of Latin theology, quoted nonbelievers saying, "See how these Christians love one another" when speaking about Christianity's practical expression of the faith.[3] Why? Because they witnessed how Christians served one another during famines or earthquakes, through poverty and persecution, and how they

> The church needs what God has given you.

---

3 Bruce L. Shelley, *Church History in Plain Language*, 5th ed. (Grand Rapids, MI: Zondervan Academic, 2021), 45.

served outside communities. Let's get back to being known by our love!

Work Together

No matter how good the basketball player is, they need a team to win. Candace Parker, LeBron James, Nikola Jokić, and Maya Moore all have two things in common: They are great players, and they are basketball champions. However, they are only champions because they had a team. As a matter of fact, they could only compete with the team. There's no five-versus-one game, and if there were, that would be highly unfair. Imagine one player guarding someone only to have to sprint as fast as they could to the other side of the court because someone passed the ball, to have to keep running because the second player with the ball passed again, and the defender was too late because a wide-open player scored. I'm exhausted just thinking about it. Or take a football game as an example. During the game, eleven players line up against another eleven players each play. But imagine if it was four players on offense versus eleven players on defense. How much scoring do you think that offensive team will accomplish? Regardless of which analogy you focus on, they both highlight what many volunteers go through in church each week.

Burnout occurs frequently because one or a few people do most of the work. Leaders, for example, find themselves planning, scheduling, laboring in prayer, hosting meetings, organizing, and developing and nurturing relationships, on top of having to clean, set up, break down, teach lessons, greet, pray with individuals, work equipment, set up lobbies, serve at events, and run administrative duties. This isn't isolated to leaders either. Some members serve in multiple areas of ministry, juggling various tasks. Imagine yourself as the leader or the member mentioned above, doing this week in and week out, on top of working a job like most people, and seeing the same members come and leave the church, not serving in any area. How would you feel? What thoughts are going through your mind?

Circumstances like the ones I share are happening across churches. But this does not have to be the case. People like you are choosing to step up and be like Christ by meeting needs, sacrificing time, talent, and treasures, and serving in love. Deciding to be the person who says "I'll do the seemingly insignificant tasks" can be the catalyst for change in your church.

Imagine your church needs someone to clean bathrooms before service begins. The church is short-handed because the normal person is not there due to burnout. Cleaning bathrooms before service means sacrificing sleep. Plus, it sounds less important than singing on the worship team, preaching, or leading a team. Greeting means standing for an extended period and keeping a smile on your face the whole

YOU'RE IMPORTANT, SO LOVINGLY SERVE WITH FAMILY

time. Sounds exhausting. So you decide to do neither. A visitor comes to the church, and because only one greeter is working, the visitor is missed. That visitor doesn't feel welcome and thinks the church is cliquish because people only talk to people they know. That same visitor decides to go to the bathroom and sees a mess. My wife and I are very bathroom conscious; if the bathrooms are poorly maintained, we usually do not stick around, no matter where we are. Perhaps this visitor feels the same about bathrooms. Now, thinking the church isn't friendly or loving and can't stay sanitary, the visitor decides to leave. This same visitor came in with a heavy heart, hoping to be encouraged and welcomed, but instead left dismayed. This visit was the final straw for them. They visited four other churches, and they all fell flat somehow. So they decide that church, maybe even Christianity, isn't for them.

Yes, I know, it is an extreme example with many variables. However, let's do a heart check to avoid missing the point. As I wrote the example, I had thoughts like "Well, greeters can't get to everyone," "Why are they being so picky?" "They must not have really wanted transformation or help if those little things turned them away or stopped them from being a Christian," and "Why didn't someone else clean the bathrooms?" These thoughts mirror Adam in the Garden in Genesis 3. Eve, deceived by Satan, ate the fruit, and she gave it to Adam, who also chose to eat the fruit. When Jehovah Elohim met them in the Garden, asking if Adam ate from the tree He told them not to eat from, Adam replied, "The woman you gave to be with me—she gave me some fruit from the tree, and I ate" (verse 12). Adam shifted the blame. Adam deflected responsibility. Adam felt he needed to distribute his guilt evenly. I believe the thoughts I had did the same. I deflected responsibility to free myself from guilt. So, yes, someone else could have volunteered to clean the bathroom, but you could have too. True, greeters can't get to everyone, and other people in the church should be friendly enough to talk with strangers. But chances improve to greet everyone if more people serve on the team. What if your act of sacrifice and service was the loving catalyst to the trajectory of that visitor's life? What if God wanted to use you in that moment?

Did that feel like I put too much pressure on a decision to serve? Honestly, that's the pressure that the few people doing most of the work feel. If that pressure made you uncomfortable, think about the people laboring week in and week out. This goes for serving outside the four walls too. There are many instances where the same people are serving during Sunday morning service, and the day before, they served all day at the food pantry or the church community outreach event. Let's help alleviate that pressure. Let's bear one another's burdens (Galatians 6:2). Let's serve in love!

CHAPTER 3

You're Important, So Add Value

I WORKED AS A SOFTWARE COMPANY support analyst for a while, and they had a great mentorship program. Employees were encouraged to sign up as mentors or mentees. Then, the program leaders paired employees with someone within the company. The pair would meet for six weeks, providing the mentee opportunities to ask questions and gain valuable insight from the mentor. Being new to the company, I signed up as a mentee because I did not have enough experience at this particular company, since I had only been there for less than a year. The program leaders paired me with someone who had been in the company for a few years, but she had less career and life experience than I did. The meetings were balanced because we shared wisdom, advice, and knowledge. We both added value to the meetings because we were open to discussing our strengths, weaknesses, successes, and mistakes. By the end of our six-week session, she encouraged me to sign up as a mentor next time.

I hope you noticed I could still add value to the conversations even though I was not the official mentor. This young woman admitted she didn't think she was a great mentor because I had more life and career experience. On the contrary, she added value because she gave me a different perspective on the company and insight into whom to network with. We both added value to each other. Titles did not matter. Positions did not matter. Knowing we had something to bring to the table and dared to share mattered. In our minds, our information and experiences may be small or not life-changing, but to someone else, what we share could change their entire life trajectory.

When serving in church, some roles appear to be greater than others, and some people perceive their role as less valuable. The onstage roles and leadership positions are exalted, while the less prominent roles are rarely recognized and respected. This perspective of certain positions being more valuable is divisive, causes envy, and can unintentionally drive people away from serving. As mentioned in the previous chapter,

Christians make up the Body of Christ, and no one part is better than the other. We're all needed, so we all have value to bring to the local church and community.

One of the most challenging parts of an interview is responding when someone says, "Tell me about yourself." I've learned that this is less an opportunity to speak about your personal life and more about how you will bring value to the company and position you applied for. It would be best to talk about your career up to this point, how you've grown professionally, what skills you've obtained, and how you apply them.

> We're all needed, so we all have value to bring to the local church & community.

For example, if you are applying for a technical position like software engineering, do not respond by talking about your random hobbies, favorite TV shows, or, honestly, your family. Yes, those things can make the interview more personable, but the interviewer is looking for something else. Unless those things tie into the position, you should respond by saying things like how you've always been interested in information technology, how you like to design websites, games, or applications, or how you're an avid reader of technology blogs and books. Why? Details of your life highlighting the skills they are searching for reveal to the interviewer that you have value to add to the company and the position.

YOU'RE IMPORTANT, SO ADD VALUE

So why is it hard for me to respond? I feel uncomfortable talking about myself or feeling like I am bragging. I'd rather show you. My dad, often my basketball coach, always told me to let my game speak for itself. There's no need to talk about my skills; I can show people on the court. I took that to heart. Maybe you relate. However, let me ease the burden for people like me. Being aware of and sharing how you can add value is okay. Read that last sentence again. I hope you feel a little lighter.

Now, sharing how you add value does not negate the need to show that you add value. I suggest you show before you tell, for a couple of reasons. One reason is that it shows humility. In Luke 14, Jesus was dining with Pharisees on the Sabbath, and He healed a man. There's much to be said about that interaction, but that's for another time. In verse 7, Jesus noticed how those invited chose places of honor for themselves. Jesus decided to tell a parable about a man who sat in a place of honor, but when the host came, the host had that man moved to the lowest place because someone more highly distinguished came to sit where the man sat. Awwkwaaarrd. So what does Jesus suggest? Verses 10 and 11 state, "But when you are invited, go and sit in the lowest place, so that when the one who invited you comes, he will say to you, 'Friend, move up higher.' You will then be honored in the presence of all the other guests. For everyone who exalts himself will be humbled, and the one who humbles himself will be exalted."

When you are about to serve in the local church, do not be so quick to boast about what you can do and how great you are at it. Instead, look for a need to help in the church and do that well. God will bring the opportunity for you to show and share that skill, talent, or gift. Finding a need and helping with it allows the Holy Spirit to nurture a servant's heart, and people will take notice of your willingness to serve and trust you with more.

I know a man who had experience teaching and preaching in other churches. When his family moved and found another church to attend, they had the opportunity to serve at the Easter event the church hosted before they even joined as members. The church needed help running the event, and this man and his wife wanted to fill that need. While he was there, he ran into the pastor. They had spoken a little bit beforehand, but he thought it would be a good idea to talk more to the leader of the church he was thinking about joining. They spoke briefly, and the man asked the pastor a question. "Is there anything I can help with?" The pastor was partially thrown off. The pastor replied, "Not many people ask that because of what could be asked of them." At that time, the event needed a specific cord for the audio system, so the man got a cord without expecting any money in return.

YOU'RE IMPORTANT, SO ADD VALUE

After a while, the pastor and the man got to know each other better, and the man had an opportunity to speak about his background and experience. The pastor mentioned that the church needed a leader in the kids' ministry and asked if the man would take on that responsibility. Without hesitation, the man said yes. A leadership opportunity was presented without the man having to force it.

A few thoughts may arise from hearing that story. Maybe leading a kids' ministry is no big deal. Perhaps it appeared the man was being manipulative by faking sincerity and scheming ways to gain position. Maybe that story is unrelatable because the pastor at your church is unapproachable. I won't tackle each of those concerns in this book, but I hope you notice the overall application of the story. The man humbly met needs that weren't his specific gift, talent, or interest, and an opportunity presented itself to come up higher. You may be the best administrator in your city, or you may know how to move a crowd better than Steven Furtick or T. D. Jakes. But for a season, are you humble enough to set up chairs or ensure there's tissue at the end of every row? The church would like to purchase better tables to serve people, but they spend money on cleaning companies. Can you spare two hours a weekend to help clean the facility? The church would like to host a trunk-or-treat event for the nearby neighborhood, but only three people have signed up. Are you willing to sacrifice your time and car for kids to enjoy a safe evening at a church and hopefully receive the Gospel? Do you have a servant's heart?

Back to our question: Why show your gifts before you share? The first reason is humility. The second reason is that showing before telling shows leadership qualities. Showing your value before saying your value reveals you lead by example. Great leaders won't just tell people what to do; they will model their expectations. Moreover, people will recognize that you bring value because you are willing to work and serve without title, position, or recognition.

NBA players from the 2008 Olympic USA basketball team share a story of leadership across different platforms. They decided to practice and work late at night to prepare for the games and then work out early in the morning too. They would get a few hours of sleep but wake up early, get dressed in full gear, and head to eat breakfast. To their surprise, Kobe Bryant was already sweating in the lobby with ice packs on his legs. When asked what was happening, Kobe admitted that he had already worked out and was about to start another workout. After telling this story during an interview, one player shared that it made

—
Showing your value before saying your value reveals you lead by example.
—

him want to be better, even though he knew he was already considered a great player.

As the great John Maxwell says, "Leadership is influence, nothing more, nothing less."[4] Kobe influenced his teammates through his actions, making them want to work hard and play better. Kobe led without telling the team they should work harder and get better at basketball; instead, he showed them that working harder can yield excellent results. Although leaders must direct people with words, their actions are just as necessary. For example, spiritual leaders not only should instruct people to fast but should be fasting too (probably more than the people they are leading). However, leading by example is not solely for positional leaders. Leading by example is an act everyone can do and benefit from. It is contagious when people see that you are gladly serving with love. Your actions can rally the team to take more initiative, increase their sacrifice, and strive for excellence.

Yes, sometimes you share what value you bring before you do anything. If that opportunity arises, be courageous and humbly share what you can do and

---

4 John Maxwell, "The Heart of Leadership: Becoming a Servant Leader," Maxwell Leadership Certified Team, https://johnmaxwell-team.com/the-heart-of-leadership/ (accessed December 16, 2024).

what God has given you. But no matter the order, dedicate yourself to serving until God moves you, and then humbly lead by example. People will see and be grateful for the value you bring.

You're Important...

All right, you've decided to look for opportunities to humbly serve the needs of the church and community as you wait for God to open doors for other opportunities. Great! So what does that look like? Where do you start? How do you prepare for the move so that when the opportunity arises, you're ready? These are all great questions to explore.

Whether you have yet to begin or are already serving, I suggest you first get to know the local church you are currently attending. Yes, you'd be surprised to know how many people attend and serve in a church where they do not know the vision or mission, doctrinal beliefs, current direction or initiatives, or leaders they may serve under. Take time to research and ask questions. It's imperative that you are in a church that is doctrinally sound and follows the basic tenets of the faith. Moreover, you must understand and know where your invested time is going.

Next, if you have not started serving, actively look for opportunities and look for the needs within the church. This may require you to step out of your comfort zone and ask other members where you can help.

Moreover, it may require you to shift your perspective on what serving looks like. For example, people usually turn down serving in the kids' ministry before even trying. I've had the privilege of serving as a kids' ministry director, and a challenging task (for any ministry, really) is gathering volunteers. I get it; working with kids can be intimidating. Plus, it can be a lot of kids. And for parents who have kids of their own to deal with, it is a lot to deal with yours plus other people's kids. I understand. But we're looking to be like Christ. I'm sure heaven was quite comfortable, but He decided to humbly come to earth, wrapping Himself in flesh experiencing the pain, hunger, fatigue, sadness, and more that humans experience.

If you don't want to lead a kids' class, can you sacrificially step out of your comfort zone and assist the main leader? Maybe help pass out snacks and activities. Or can you work the check-in system (or establish one)? Can you communicate with parents by calling or emailing, asking what they may need prayer for or if their kids need help in school? More often than not, someone hears "kids' ministry" and rests on the thought that they don't know how to work with kids. Someone hears "greeter team" and rests on the thought that they don't get along with people. Do not hear about a serving opportunity and immediately rest on what you think it will be like. Instead of making choices based on what you can't do, won't do, or don't do, make choices based on what you can do, what you will do, and what you are willing to learn.

Local churches have many opportunities to make an impact and help—not an entity, business, or building, but children, women, and men who need Jesus just like you. Your time, talent, and treasure are welcomed, from megachurches to home churches, from large parachurch ministries to programs looking to bring Christ through serving local needs. Adonai gave you thoughts, ideas, abilities, gifts, and talents that can be used to change your sphere of influence and beyond. The question is, How will you use what you have?

. . . So Add Value

I've encountered many great leaders. I can list many reasons for that statement, but one reason is that they are resourceful and share their resources. One leader in particular introduced me to profile assessments. One assessment is called DiSC®. DiSC® is a personal assessment tool used to help improve teamwork, communication, and productivity.[5] It's a fantastic tool that provides insight into workstyle preferences, can determine how someone would interact with other people, and provides insight into work habits, among other things. Something similar is the CliftonStrengths assessment. The assessment measures your unique talents—your natural patterns of thinking, feeling, and

---

5   "What Is DiSC®?" Disc Profile, https://www.discprofile.com/what-is-disc (accessed December 10, 2024).

behaving—and categorizes them into the thirty-four CliftonStrengths themes.[6]

I share these tools because these insights are ways you can add value to yourself and where you serve. They add value because knowing your strengths and weaknesses, the hows and whys you think or react a certain way, and how you interact with others increases your self-awareness. Self-awareness is conscious knowledge of one's character, feelings, motives, and desires.[7] This conscious knowledge aids decision-making and interaction with those you serve or serve with. Moreover, it helps you communicate with leaders who you are, what you bring to the table regarding serving, and how they can help you grow in the areas you're interested in growing.

For example, one of my strengths from the CliftonStrengths assessment is Intellection: "People exceptionally talented in the Intellection theme are characterized by their intellectual activity. They are introspective and appreciate intellectual discussions."[8] When I use my strength, I add value by sharing thoughtful ideas and strategies, or I easily engage with

---

[6] "Learn How the CliftonStrengths Assessment Works," Gallup.com, https://www.gallup.com/cliftonstrengths/en/253676/how-cliftonstrengths-works.aspx (accessed December 10, 2024).

[7] Oxford Languages, s.v. "self-awareness," accessed December 10, 2024, via Google search.

[8] "An Introduction to the Intellection® CliftonStrengths Theme," Gallup.com, https://www.gallup.com/cliftonstrengths/en/252284/intellection-theme.aspx (accessed December 10, 2024).

people about their struggles, hopes, dreams, or plans in life. At first, I didn't recognize this as a strength. Partly I wanted to be humble as best as I could. But then I became concerned that I wasn't sharing or engaging enough in meetings. I thought people might believe I had nothing to contribute, or other negative thoughts. This test helped me become aware that I take time to process what I hear, formulate deep thoughts, and then articulate my thoughts at another time. Instead of forcing incomplete thoughts or never sharing, I now focus on completely listening and taking notes during conversations to confidently share what I've thought about, at the best opportune time, which can help the church and people.

If you've never taken one of these assessments, I highly encourage you to take one of these or something similar. However, these assessments do not provide a complete view of who you are and your strengths. I also recommend asking the people who know you best. This can be your family, friends, pastors, managers, teachers, or anyone else who can provide another perspective. Ask them what they've noticed you're good at or interested in. What have you helped them or others with before? Where are areas of growth? Be aware of the value of other perspectives, especially from those who will provide honest feedback.

The last and most important point is to model and pattern your life after Christ. Take a moment to look at Mark 1:17. Take another moment and think about Jesus' first two words, "Follow me." Jesus is speaking to Simon (Peter) and Andrew, calling them to be His disciples. He calls them to watch and experience His way of life, look to Him as Master, and begin to model and pattern their life after His. You have the same call. We are to observe and do what Jesus did. Specific to how you will add value, I implore you to steadily increase the quality and quantity of prayer, Scripture reading, and fasting. Why? These are means of transformation.

First, look back at Mark 1:17. Jesus says He will make the disciples fishers of men. That is God doing the work. Paul states in Romans 8:29 that God predestined to conform you to the image of His Son, Jesus Christ. That is God doing the work. Philippians 1:6 proclaims that God will complete the good work He started in you. That is God doing the work. So if God transforms, what do you do? How do prayer, Scripture reading, and fasting help to add value? By engaging in these disciplines, you are allowing God to do this transformative work, shaping and molding your mind and character to mirror Christ and helping you to grow in the knowledge of God, which is where we find everything we need for life and godliness (2 Peter 1:3). There's a song that declares that what the world needs is love. Although love is great, I would change it to say that what the world needs now is Christ, who is love. The Holy Spirit makes you more like Christ, and the spiritual disciplines are one way He does. And as you use your strengths and gifts by sacrificially giving your time, talent, and treasure through the ways of Christ, you will add value to yourself and others that lasts beyond this life.

CHAPTER 4

You're Important, So Be Healthy

HAVE YOU EVER FOUND YOURSELF in the zone, whether creating a presentation on the computer, working out, or practicing on a musical instrument, and suddenly you feel pain or discomfort? You're likely experiencing overexertion. My most recent experience was at my previous job where I had to close many cases. During month-end or quarter-end (the end of a month or the end of a quarter within the year), cases multiplied, and I had to ensure I sped up my pace to close cases. I found myself typing emails, notating calls, and navigating our system back to back to back with no breaks in between. Then, out of nowhere, a shocking pain in my wrist immediately ended my consistent workflow. No amount of rubbing, stretching, or clenching would take that pain away. I was experiencing overexertion.

Healthline.com describes overexertion as when you push yourself too hard, involving physical or mental (and I would add spiritual) effort beyond your current abilities.[9] The causes include repetitive movements, improper technique, sudden movements, and prolonged activities. Pain, fatigue, and injury are a few general symptoms. Nevertheless, avoiding or at least lowering your chances of suffering from overexertion is possible. This includes stretching and warming up muscles, strengthening joints by working out, and rest. No matter your age, developing these healthy habits is a good idea so you can continue to perform at your best. However, avoiding overexertion is not limited to your physical or mental health. The same principles apply spiritually as well.

Burnout is a common symptom of overexertion when serving the local church. Burnout is when someone has reached their capacity for serving because they've gone too long without rest, they've juggled too many responsibilities, or life has become overwhelming because of church and life outside of church. This

---

9 "The Signs of Overexertion and How to Protect Yourself from Injury and Burnout," Healthline.com, December 8, 2020, https://www.healthline.com/health/overexertion (accessed December 16, 2024).

appears to be solely physical or mental; however, burnout has spiritual origins. The mind and physical body are affected, and the pain or fatigue is real. But just like sneezing and runny noses prove you are already infected, feeling burnt out is a symptom that you've already overexerted yourself beforehand and your spirit has suffered in some way.

Generally, serving feels good, and people like to serve. Moreover, church leaders love to have willing volunteers who are eager to give their time, talent, and treasure to the church because, as Jesus said, "The harvest is abundant, but the workers are few" (Matthew 9:37). But what can happen is that realistic need combined with the deceptive feeling of obligation propels people forward in an endless cycle of serving. They eventually overexert themselves and get burnt out. This can look like a volunteer who teaches a kids' class every Sunday with little to no help, but since there's a lack of volunteers, they cannot take a break. Or someone who serves in various ministries but is pressured by leadership to continue serving because they cannot afford for you to stop, or they deceitfully make that person feel guilty for needing a break. Or someone dedicated to the church who has placed unnecessary pressure on themselves to keep serving, although life outside the church is weighing them down.

Too often, the church takes most or all the blame for causing burnout. There are cases where the church is at fault and leaders are the culprit. In other cases, I believe it will serve you best to investigate and identify the cause of burnout instead of automatically blaming the local church and its leaders. Investigating takes asking and answering questions that can be challenging. For example, before you began serving, was your serving capacity discussed? Did you communicate how much time you could serve in a month or for that quarter or year? Did anyone talk about breaks or sabbaticals? Have you established spiritual, mental, and physical disciplines and routines that keep you healthy? Do you actively recruit volunteers or leave that up to the leader? Investigating and identifying the root causes of burnout is intimidating, but going through the process will help you avoid burnout. More importantly, asking these questions before you begin serving is better in order to avoid burning out altogether.

You're Important . . .

A typical example of taking care of yourself before attempting to help others is the oxygen mask in an airplane emergency. Before takeoff, the flight crew explains what each passenger should do if there's an emergency and the oxygen masks are released. To paraphrase, you must secure your mask before assisting someone else with their mask. Why? They do not want you running out of oxygen because you won't be able to help anyone else. Imagine you have a child, and the masks are released. You do your best to secure their mask successfully; however, you become unconscious before securing your mask. Who's watching over your child? The idea is to be at your best to successfully and continuously help others.

The metaphor of putting your mask on before helping someone else supports the idea of self-care. Self-care is the concept that every individual needs to find things in life that make them feel good, replenished, and healthy so they can be productive and help others. Although self-care can be idolized when priorities are not aligned correctly, the overall idea is helpful. Often, humans prioritize their physical or emotional self before others or their emotions over the Holy Spirit. This is when self-care can become an idol, and we begin to live selfishly but disguise it behind the term self-care. For example, we decide to give less time to discipleship or attend church less because we must keep our self-care routine. Or we feel a certain way when the Holy Spirit challenges us to give financially because it'll take away from our self-care activities. Please understand that I am not against self-care. However, I want to introduce the idea of soul-care. Soul-care should accompany self-care and keep self-care in its proper place.

Soul-Care and Self-Care

Soul-care and self-care sound similar and should be practiced together; nevertheless, they differ. The simple difference is that soul-care concerns the inner person, and self-care concerns the outer person. Allow me to explain. In Paul's second letter to the Corinthians, he describes how his present suffering (persecution and hardship as an apostle) doesn't compare to what awaits him in heaven; the same is true for all believers. Paul states, "Therefore we do not give up. Even though our outer person is being destroyed, our inner person is being renewed day by day" (2 Corinthians 4:16). Let us begin with the inner person.

The inner person is the soul and spirit (differing arguments exist regarding dichotomy versus trichotomy that this book won't discuss). The inner person includes the mind, will, and emotions and is being sanctified (2 Thessalonians 2:13) and renewed (Romans 12:2). By the power and work of the Holy Spirit, spiritual disciplines (Scripture reading and meditation, prayer, fasting, and serving are a few), fellowship with other believers, and pastoral counsel, our soul is renewed, refreshed, and reinvigorated.

Living a Christian life is not easy. All followers of Christ are in spiritual warfare, all face temptations, and all go through trials and tribulations. And since we experience these things, we can experience stress, weariness, loneliness, and despair that burden our souls. This is one reason why soul-care is essential. We can receive peace as we're in prayer (Philippians 4:4–7), we can experience encouragement and support as we fellowship with believers (Hebrews 10:24–25), and we can acquire guidance from pastoral counsel (Hebrews 13:17). So soul-care is focused on the immaterial unseen aspects of the believer. Praise God for graciously giving us these means to help followers of Christ mature spiritually and renew the inner self.

Self-care is broader and includes the body and the soul/spirit. Why both body and soul? As mentioned before, most of the examples listed can help increase the immaterial aspects, like peace and joy. Regarding the body, Scripture states that physical training has limited benefits (1 Timothy 4:8), but that still means it has benefits. It's essential to take care of the temples of the Holy Spirit and honor God with our bodies (1 Corinthians 6:19–20)—self-care concerns how we take care of our physical body to honor God. Getting proper rest (actual sleep or taking necessary breaks from working), exercising, and maintaining good nutritional habits are examples of self-care; each looks different for everyone. Self-care also includes engaging in activities that energize or relax you. Playing sports, reading, creating art or music,

> Soul-care is focused on the immaterial unseen aspects of the believer

watching movies, and cooking are other examples of self-care. Self-care is important because God has given humanity life for enjoyment, and we primarily enjoy life through the five senses (Ecclesiastes 3:12–13). From work to parenting to generally navigating through life's ups and downs, practicing self-care is okay and beneficial to practice.

Keep Them Together

As mentioned earlier, soul-care and self-care go hand in hand. Early Christians faced a looming worldview called Gnosticism. One aspect of the Gnostic belief is that the material world, including the body, is evil, and they overemphasize the spiritual realm over the natural. However, it is imperative to know and remember that God created the physical world and proclaimed it good (Genesis 1). In His sovereignty, God chose to have humans inhabit a body to worship Him. And though plagued by the consequences of sin (decay and death), the body is still an instrument to be used for righteousness (Romans 6:13).

Therefore, practicing soul-care and self-care can be viewed as loving God. Why? Jesus stated that the greatest commandment is to "Love the Lord your God with all your heart, with all your soul, with all your mind, and with all your strength" (Mark 12:30). This means we are to pursue, submit, and honor God with our whole being, body, and soul. When focused on soul-care, we focus on loving God by spiritually maturing and developing a closer relationship with Him. When focused on self-care, we help ourselves maintain a healthy state of being to actively honor God. Practicing both promotes a healthy Christian life. Think about how difficult it would be to serve at church, work a job, read Scripture, pray, and have time for family if you do not prioritize getting enough sleep every night. Or imagine you struggle with the same sinful habit because you do not fast, have not replaced the bad habit with a good habit, and have not sought accountability. Or picture your stress level and how fast you could reach burnout if all you do and think about is work (whether serving or occupation) without taking time to do things you enjoy and rejuvenating your soul through praising and worshiping Adonai. Do any of these examples sound appealing to you? I assume not. So do not wait any longer. Develop the rhythm and practice of soul-care and self-care and live a healthy Christian life now.

> Develop the rhythm & practice of soul-care and self-care and live a healthy Christian life now.

. . . So Be Healthy

Adonai cares about our whole being. Our Lord provides nourishment for the physical body (1 Kings

19:5–7) and the soul (Psalm 23:3). This is evident in the life of Christ, for example, when He fed the five thousand (Mark 6:30–44). First, we enter the scene where the disciples have returned from their missionary journey. Jesus sent the disciples out to preach repentance to Israel, heal the sick, and cast out demons (Mark 6:7–13). When they returned, Jesus did not tell them "good job but keep going" because they had momentum. Instead, Jesus said, "Come away by yourselves to a remote place and rest for a while" (Mark 6:31). Soon after, Jesus taught the multitude of over five thousand people, providing spiritual food. Afterward, He made sure they had physical nutrition by multiplying fish and loaves.

Be aware of what Jesus reveals to us in this text. We should serve in love and obedience to Christ. We should also take time to rest and take care of ourselves. If our Lord cares for our whole being, we should too. As you look to serve or continue serving, evaluate your life and honestly answer these questions: Are you a healthy disciple of Christ? Are you practicing soul- and self-care? Are you serving faithfully but also taking the time to sit under the preached Word of God? Are you taking care of your temple by eating healthy and exercising? If you are practicing soul- and self-care, are you encouraging others to do the same?

I think it's important to remind ourselves not to abuse and idolize healthiness. We must be honest with ourselves and those we serve with and under. When we choose to serve, we take on responsibilities and expectations that we should honor. Serve with integrity. If you can serve, do so. If you cannot, communicate with your leader. Be open and honest, and work with your leader to develop a cadence that works for you and the ministry. The goal of being a healthy disciple of Christ is to become more like Christ. Jesus taught and exemplified caring for the well-being of others. We show we care and love our leaders by giving our best and allowing them to lead well and not experience the stress and burnout we're trying to avoid. Let us obey our Lord and love others as we love ourselves.

Would you like to book Herman as a speaker at your next event, training, or conference?

Please email hbj@royaltylanepublishing.com
or visit www.royaltylanepublishing.com.

www.ingramcontent.com/pod-product-compliance
Lightning Source LLC
Chambersburg PA
CBHW072016060426
42446CB00043B/2572